Contents

– An Introduction to Streptocarpus –

The admirable qualities of streptocarpus – long-lasting, free-flowering and easy-to-grow – have made them really popular in recent years, as people have come to appreciate their value as appealing plants for the greenhouse, conservatory or house. They have been in cultivation for a long time, and are far more widely available now than they used to be. Most good garden centres stock a range of modern rather than the old seed-raised hybrids. These modern streptocarpus, hybrids and cultivars, with their showy flowers come in a multitude of forms and colours, the latter ranging from pinks and reds to blues and deep purples, as well as whites. The plants can have few large flowers or masses of dainty little ones, and they can be either single or double.

Streptocarpus belong to the family Gesneriaceae. This large family of very advanced plants occurs throughout the world, but mainly in the tropics and sub-tropics. The members of the family are very diverse, and often highly specialised. Often it is hard to identify gesneriads but the flower and not the plant habit is the diagnostic feature. The flower has a number of characteristics amongst which are bilateral symmetry, five-fused sepals and five petals fused to form a tube. Familiar members of this family, as well as *Streptocarpus*, are African violets (*Saintpaulia*) and the florists' gloxinia (*Sinningia*). Many other members of the family, though not so well known, also make excellent cultivated plants, e.g. *Columnea*, *Achimene*, *Alsobia*, *Aeschynanthus*, *Kohleria* and *Nematanthus*.

The genus *Streptocarpus* is divided into two sections, sub-genera, one being *Streptocarpus*, and the other *Streptocarpella*. The former group is the one that is more familiar, where there appears to be no visible stem, and the leaves develop at ground level. This group can again be split into plants that only have a single leaf – the so called 'unifoliates'; and those that have a rosette of leaves – the 'rosulates'.

UNIFOLIATES AND ROSULATES

The unifoliates are not such appealing plants as the rosulates for general cultivation: they are of more interest to the specialist grower. For the one leaf, that grows from one of the two seed-

Streptocarpus 'Kim' displayed on the authors' stand at a Chelsea Flower Show (see p. 56)

Unifoliate *Streptocarpus wittei* growing wild near Chowo in Malawi

A streptocarpus plant forming abscission layers in the autumn

leaves, or cotyledons, can become very large, up to 2 ft (60 cm) in length and 6 in. (15 cm) wide, and can look rather tatty. Eventually they produce a mass of flowers, set seed and then usually die. The unifoliates can hybridise with the rosulates and have played an important role in the development of modern hybrids.

The modern hybrids are rosulates and many species have contributed to their make-up. Their growth pattern is very unusual in that the leaf grows constantly from the base, and as it gets older the far end dies back. Sometimes a distinct line can be seen across the leaf, an abscission zone, where the tip – the older part – dies away and drops off.

The flowering stems which bear the inflorescences arise at the base of the leaf in succession. This means that each leaf may have on it, all at the same time, inflorescences that have finished flowering and have set seed, young ones that are in the process of flowering and, furthest out from the centre of the plant, still younger flowering stems that are just beginning to curl upwards.

Because of the appearance of the rosette of leaves, plants are sometimes known as Cape primroses. Indeed when not in flower the plant is not unlike a primula. Streptocarpus are not, however, related to primroses and this common name creates an erroneous impression of the relationship between the plant and its cultivation. It is therefore preferable to use the proper name.

The name *Streptocarpus* is derived from Greek and means 'twisted fruit' (*streptos*, twisted, and *carpus*, fruit); if a ripe fruit is examined, it will indeed be seen that it opens up like a spring, to release the dust-like seed.

STEMMED STREPTOCARPUS

The second main group, the sub-genus *Streptocarpella*, are quite different in appearance from the first group in that they have a visible stem, along which the leaves and the flowering stems are arranged. This group – referred to as the stemmed streptocarpus – is not as well known in cultivation, though some species and cultivars such as *Streptocarpus saxorum* and S. 'Concord Blue' are well worth growing.

Plants of this sub-genus have a different chromosome number to the sub-genus *Streptocarpus*, so that crossings can not be made between the two sub-genera.

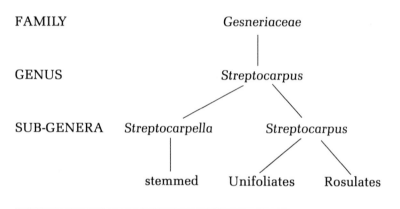

FAMILY   *Gesneriaceae*

GENUS   *Streptocarpus*

SUB-GENERA   *Streptocarpella*   *Streptocarpus*

                  stemmed   Unifoliates   Rosulates

Streptocarpus saxorum is one of the stemmed species (see above)

Streptocarpus eylesii subsp. *brevistylus*, a unifoliate, growing in Malawi

DISTRIBUTION

Streptocarpus occur mainly in Africa, including Madagascar, with just a few stemmed species, sub-genus *Streptocarpella*, found in the Far East. The rest of the stemmed species grow in tropical Africa, from Sierra Leone in the west right across to the Indian Ocean, and on Madagascar.

The sub-genus *Streptocarpus* occurs in East Africa, its range forming a band from the Cape as far north as Ethiopia and westward to Angola. They also occur in Madagascar. However, as one goes northwards the number of species declines. These plants grow in the mountains and forests, live on rocky outcrops, stream sides and by cave entrances. They thrive in conditions that are shady and moist in summer and where there is good drainage. The winters are mostly dry, but occasionally plants have to endure some frost. It is during winter that the leaves may wilt and die back at the tips.

History

The first species to be introduced into Europe was *Streptocarpus rexii* in 1826, which was named in honour of the King, George IV, and first flowered at The Royal Botanic Gardens, Kew, the following year. Other species were introduced in 1855 and work commenced on making crosses. Gradually more and more species were introduced and included in the breeding programme.

Most of the species used in breeding were in the blue, mauve or white range but a landmark occurred in 1886 when an unifoliate, *S. dunnii* was brought into the crossing. This plant has bright red flowers and although not very useful itself as an ornamental, it enabled colour to be transferred into the rosulate type of habit.

Crossing continued at Kew and at the nursery of Messrs Veitch. All the time the habit was brought back to the *S. rexii* type and, by the turn of the century, the complicated mixture was named *S. × hybridus*. Crossings had also been carried out in France at one time, but this appears to have ceased and has played no part in the development of today's range of plants.

During the 1930s W. J. C. Lawrence at the John Innes Institute, Merton, Greater London, was using streptocarpus in research on breeding behaviour. Though not primarily trying to breed new hybrids, he did get a good one called 'Merton Blue', which, when crossed with a multiflowered species, *S. johannis*, produced the very popular 'Constant Nymph', which was introduced to the market in 1947.

'Constant Nymph' can truly be called the first of the modern multiflowered, flat-faced streptocarpus. This plant became quite popular in the UK but was not grown much by nurserymen. However, it did become very popular commercially in the Netherlands and it was in a nursery there that a white sport occurred which was called 'Maassen's White'. This is identical to 'Constant Nymph' except that it is unable to manufacture the purple pigment, hence the flowers are white and the flower stalks are green. 'Constant Nymph' and 'Maassen's White' were treated chemically with X-rays at a Dutch research station to give a range of mutations. From 'Constant Nymph' several variations were named, including 'Blue Nymph' and 'Mini Nymph'. 'Maassen's White' gave rise to a

---

Streptocarpus 'Paula' is a John Innes hybrid (see p. 58)

Above: Aptly named *Streptocarpus* 'Snow White' (see p. 59)
Below: *Streptocarpus* 'Albatross' (see p. 50)

Streptocarpus primulifolius subsp. *formosus* (see p. 47)

small plant, 'Snow White', and the bigger, more robust 'Albatross'. This latter is a tetraploid, which means that the cells have four sets of chromosomes instead of the usual two (known as diploid).

In the early 1970s Gavin Brown at the John Innes Institute, realising that 'Constant Nymph' was an excellent plant, repeated the cross with *S. johannis* and other coloured forms of *S. × hybridus* to obtain plants of the same habit as 'Constant Nymph', but in a wide range of colours. The results over the following few years were spectacular. The first generation of plants gave some excellent blues and mauves, two of which were named: 'Louise' and 'Paula'. This generation of plants was allowed to set seed, and it was in the next generation that a brilliant range of colours developed. Of the vast number produced, a few were selected for naming, and some of these are still among the best available today, e.g. 'Tina' (see front cover and page 60).

Other species have also been used in breeding in recent years. *S. primulifolius* subsp. *formosus* has been used to give large, veined flowers such as in 'Sandra' (see pages 58 and 59). In Britain crossing

work continues at Dibleys' Nurseries in North Wales, producing such cultivars as 'Amanda' (see pages 50 and 51) and 'Kim' (see pages 4 and 56). One complaint about streptocarpus is that they can have excessively large leaves, but 'Kim' is small and compact.

Another important breakthrough was the discovery at Dibleys' Nurseries of a sport of S. *johannis*, in which the flowers are larger, of a darker blue and carried on a much shorter stem than the species. This was called 'Falling Stars' (see pages 32, 35 and 54), and has itself been used in further crosses.

Breeding goes on in the United States where a wide range of colours and types have been produced, though the multiflowered habit is not so pronounced as it is among British cultivars. Some of the American plants, however, are nice and compact, like 'Athena'. The Americans have also given us the first truly double strepto-carpus, 'Rosebud'. New cultivars have also been produced by plant breeders in Europe. The very deep purple 'Elsi' is an example of their work.

As well as through deliberate crosses, new plants may also arise by chance mutations. These occur not infrequently, though, as with plants produced by crossing, the majority are of no commercial value. A few, however, are good enough to use, such as 'Ruby' which is a sport of 'Cynthia', but lacking the blue tinge; and 'Gloria' (see pages 32 and 54), which is a pink form of 'Falling Stars'.

With more and more hybrids and species being used in the breeding programme, the range of colours and forms should continue to increase, and the future looks very bright indeed for these beautiful pot plants.

Above: *Streptocarpus* 'Athena' is a very free-flowering and compact plant (see p. 50)
Below: *Streptocarpus* 'Rosebud' was the first fully double cultivar to be developed (see p. 58)

Cultivation

As with all plants, streptocarpus will grow and flower best in conditions that are as near to their natural habitat as possible. Thus in summer, they like dappled sunlight. If the light is too bright and the temperature hot, the leaves and flowers will become burnt and shrivelled. If the light is not sufficient, the plants may make extra-large leaves and will fail to flower.

WHERE TO GROW STREPTOCARPUS

In the greenhouse these conditions will be satisfied by growing the plants on the staging, but with shading of some kind over them. This can be either plastic netting, slatted blinds or the shading that is painted onto the glass. A moveable shading has the advantage in that it can be opened early and late in the day, and closed in the middle of the day, or left open on dull days. This ensures optimum growing conditions. A north-facing conservatory is a suitable home for streptocarpus in summer. If it faces in any other direction, the same shading precautions will be needed as in a greenhouse.

Good ventilation is essential and as the temperature reaches about 68°F (20°C) the vents should be opened. Some conservatories lack sufficient ventilation; remember when buying a conservatory it will be a distinct advantage if extra ventilation can be added, always bearing security in mind. However, the plants can withstand higher temperatures for a short period providing they are not in strong sunlight.

In the house an east- or west-facing window is the ideal position. This gives some early morning or evening sunlight but will avoid the burning mid-day sun. A north-facing window will be suitable, providing it is large so that plenty of light is admitted. A south-facing windowsill should be avoided, though if plants are set back a little into the room this can prove satisfactory. Plants in rooms facing in any direction other than south should be placed on the windowsill, since further into the room the light will be insufficient and lack of light is one common cause of plants not reaching their full flowering potential. Remember that plants are very sensitive to

Streptocarpus 'Ruby' (see p. 58)

light. Although our eyes adjust readily to different light levels, it is hard for us to appreciate how much the light intensity drops as we move away from a window.

During the winter (November to February) the plants will stand all the light that they can be given. Remove all shading in the greenhouse or conservatory, and in the house place the plants, if possible, in a south-facing window.

The stemmed varieties, sub-genus *Streptocarpella*, need a higher temperature than the rosette types in winter, and they require a minimum of 50°F (10°C).

POTTING

Streptocarpus plants grow well in a standard peat-based compost. Coco-fibre composts are also suitable, though feeding may have to commence earlier. John Innes Compost No. 2 is also satisfactory, though the more open peat and fibre composts give better root development.

Established young cuttings need to be potted into a 3.5 in (10 cm) pot. They can stay in this until the roots completely fill the pot, then move them into a 5 in (13 cm) one. A shallow pot is better than a full depth container. Continental pots are more squat than the traditional British pot, and thus more suitable for streptocarpus. Throughout this book the metric measurement refers to continental shape, and the imperial measurement to the nearest equivalent British pot.

A plant put into a smaller pot in the spring will need to go into a bigger size later the same summer. A plant first potted up after midsummer can stay in the same container until the following spring, and then be put into the bigger pot when growth commences. It is possible to grow really large plants in quite small pots provided they are fed properly. Never over-pot a plant: it is better for it to be slightly root-bound than over-potted.

In the following years a slightly larger pot can be used, repotting each spring. Though plants can live for many years, after three or four years it is better to take cuttings to start new plants, and throw the old plant away, once you are sure your cuttings have rooted satisfactorily. You will then have vigorous young plants again, and these will prove more floriferous than older plants.

WATERING

Water with care. As with most houseplants, incorrect watering is a common cause of failure. The plants need plenty of water on hot

This Gold Medal winning display at Chelsea has 'Falling Stars' as its centrepiece (see p. 54)

sunny days, but much less at other times. Only water when the plant needs it, water thoroughly and then leave until the compost is almost dry. It does not matter whether the plant is watered from above or below, but it must on no account be left standing in the water after the compost has become wet. Also, do not get water on the leaves in bright light or they will become marked. During the winter, in low temperatures, very little water is needed. Provided the plants are kept on the dry side they can withstand a temperature as low as 41°F (5°C). More water is needed by plants in a warmer situation, such as a living room. Central heating will do them no harm at all provided they are not directly over a hot radiator.

FEEDING

After potting plants into new compost they do not require feeding for about a month, but after this they require regular feeding during the growing season (March to October). If using a liquid fertiliser, feeding is required about once a week. However, it is easier to use slow-release fertiliser tablets that only need inserting below the soil level, one tablet every month for small plants, or as recommended by the manufacturer. For larger plants that are in a 5 in (13 cm) pot, two tablets will be needed each month. Use fertiliser that has a high potash content. This will encourage flowering rather than too much vegetative growth. The same fertiliser can be used throughout the growing season. On any fertiliser container are three figures giving the nitrogen, phosphate and potash content (N:P:K). Always ensure the last figure is about double the first figure; the proportions should be about 1:1:2. If you use a feed with the first figure the highest (which means it is high in nitrogen) you will get large lush leaves, but not much flower.

During the winter do not feed at all, but by March when new growth starts to appear, gradually commence feeding again.

DEADHEADING AND LEAF CARE

Always remove the dead flowers, and once a complete inflorescence (flower spike) has finished flowering cut it off at the base. This will encourage new flowers to develop, as well as making the plant neater. When a flower has finished, the petals may drop off. Therefore, always pick the petals off the plant if they have fallen on to the leaves. If they are left, they may become infected with grey mould, or botrytis, which will spread into the leaf, turning it mouldy. This problem can be especially troublesome in the later part of the growing season when conditions are cooler and more damp.

As leaves get old they may die back at the tips. This occurs particularly in winter, and as explained earlier, a distinct abscission line may be visible. This is perfectly normal with streptocarpus and is not caused, as is sometimes thought, by contact with an object. Just break off the dead end; this causes no harm to the plant whatsoever.

FLOWERING

Flowers of streptocarpus are excellent for cutting: they are long lasting and can be made into lovely displays. The plants have the great advantage that they will go on producing more flowers. Even if you take off all the inflorescences, in a few days the plant will be back in flower again.

Plants can be made to grow and flower the year round if they are given light of sufficient duration and intensity, and of the correct spectrum. Fluorescent tubes can be bought that have been developed specially to improve plant growth, but these are more expensive than warm-white tubes; and the latter do the job just as well. If two or three tubes are fixed about 18 in. (45 cm) above plants on a bench 3–4 ft (90–120 cm) wide, and turned on for approximately 14 hours a day, plants will grow and flower beautifully the year round. They will need to be kept at 59°F to 68°F (15°C to 20°C). This is a technique that is popular in the USA, providing flowers in the home throughout the year. So far this method has not caught on in Britain to any great extent, but it is a rewarding procedure and should be considered by plant-lovers.

Some cultivars seem to lose their vigour and flower less freely if kept for a long time. It is therefore recommended to take cuttings from plants once they reach three or four years old. Keep the old plants until the new plants are established, as an insurance policy.

Streptocarpus 'Lisa' (see pp. 36 and 56)

Propagation

Streptocarpus belong to a small group of plants that can be propagated from a single leaf. The young plants that develop will, of course, as with any method of vegetative propagation, be identical to the parent, so that if the grower wants to maintain a cultivar it must be propagated this way. Seeds will generally not breed true.

LEAF CUTTINGS

Cuttings can be taken at any time when the parent plant has a supply of young leaves. In practice this usually means spring or summer. Old leaves are not suitable material for propagation as they lack vigour. The leaf chosen should be taken from near the centre of the plant, and be green and fresh-looking along its whole length, not yellow or dying back at the tip. Snap the leaf off at its base. The leaf can then be treated in a number of ways, dependent on the grower's skill and the number of young plants required.

The easiest way is to insert the base of the leaf about 1 in. (2.5 cm) deep into the compost in a small pot, 3 in. (8 cm) in size, and water thoroughly. Suitable compost is either a proprietary compost specially produced for cuttings or a peat-based compost mixed in equal proportions with medium-grade vermiculite. Water thoroughly, then ideally place the pot in a propagating case. Alternatively put a polythene bag over the pot with sticks inserted to hold the polythene clear of the leaf cutting.

Place the propagating case or pot in a bright place but not in the full sun. After about four weeks the leaf should have rooted, and after about another four weeks a tuft of leaves will appear at the base of the cutting.

Either gradually increase the ventilation in the propagating case, or slit the polythene bag a little at a time for several days until it is finally removed, so that the young plant becomes gradually inured to the room temperature. As the pot becomes full of roots, repot into a larger pot, $3\frac{1}{2}$ in. (10 cm), filled with potting-compost – John Innes potting compost number 2 or a soilless equivalent. Start

Young plants developing at the base of leaf cuttings

feeding after a few weeks. The plant should start flowering after about another three months.

If several plants are wanted, the leaf being used as a cutting can be cut transversely into several pieces, each about 2 in. (5 cm) in length. The number obtained from one leaf will obviously depend on the size of the leaf chosen. Each piece is then treated as above, making sure the sections are planted the correct way up, i.e. place the basal end which was the point of attachment, in the compost. Instead of using pots, a propagating cell pack divided into a number of sections can be used, putting a piece of leaf in each cell. Subsequently, treat as described for the individual leaf, above, potting up each rooted cutting into an individual 3½ in. (10 cm) pot.

If a large number of plants are required, then choose a broad leaf and cut it cleanly down either side of the midrib. The midrib is then discarded and each half of the leaf, cut face down, is set into compost in a seed tray, the cut face being just covered in compost.

Again, treat as described above. However, if conditions are not ideal, leaves are more liable to rot and die by this method which is more suitable for an experienced grower who has the use of a propagating case. As young plants will grow along the length of the leaf, a single leaf can give several dozen plantlets.

When the young plantlets are well established, i.e. the leaves are 1 to 2 in. (2.5 to 5 cm) in length, the old leaf can be carefully teased

Rows of young plants growing from the cut face of leaves cut longitudinally either side of the midrib

24

from the compost, along with its row of plantlets. Break the old leaf into chunks with a few plantlets on each, taking care not to damage the network of fibrous roots, and plant each section into potting compost in a 3.5 in. (10 cm) pot. Ensure the plantlets are not planted too deeply or too shallowly in the new compost, but at the same height as they were previously. Water thoroughly. A light misting of water will help for a few days until the plants are established in their new pots. Alternatively, plant the small clumps of plantlets into sections of a propagating cell pack, and allow them to grow on for a month or two before potting up. After a few weeks the parent leaf will probably wither and die.

It is possible to cut leaves into other shapes to use as cuttings, but there are no additional benefits: the above methods give the best results.

PROPAGATING STEMMED STREPTOCARPUS
(subsp. *Streptocarpella*)

These plants can easily be propagated from a shoot. Cut off the end of a shoot about 3 in. (8 cm) long. Remove the lowest pair of leaves, and discard. Dipping the cut tip of the stem in a hormone rooting powder may encourage root development, especially if conditions are not ideal. Use a mixture of equal parts of peat-based compost

Streptocarpus candidus (see p. 46)

25

and medium-grade vermiculite, as described above for propagating from leaf cuttings. Insert each cutting in a small, 3 in. (9 cm) pot and cover with a polythene bag held clear of the cutting by two or three short canes. Place in a warm, light position, but not in full sun. After two to three weeks the cuttings will start to look perky, and if given a gentle twitch will be found to be fixed firmly into the soil. Gradually remove the polythene by splitting open the bag a little more each day. Once the pot is filled with roots move the plant into a larger, $3\frac{1}{2}$ in. (10 cm) pot, using a soilless potting compost.

A heated propagating case set at about 68°F (20°C) will ensure rapid rooting of cuttings. If a number of plants are wanted, then the use of a multicell pack instead of pots is a better alternative. Again, once the cuttings are well rooted move each into a $3\frac{1}{2}$ in. (10 cm) pot, or, for a more spectacular effect, pot up several cuttings into a single pot. The number of cuttings required depends on the size of pot and the speed with which you require to achieve a mature plant. Obviously the more cuttings used, the quicker a more mature-looking plant will be produced. Commercial growers usually place three cuttings in a 5 in. (13 cm) pot. For trailing species such as S. saxorum, a number of plants can be placed in a hanging basket. If a bushy plant is desired, stopping the plant by pinching out the tip will encourage the development of side shoots.

RAISING FROM SEED

Plants can of course be grown from seed. However, only species will come true from seed, the hybrids and cultivars will generally give an unpredictable mixture of colours and forms. That is not to say some of the offspring will not be interesting; it is impossible to tell what will occur exactly. Red-flowered plants will probably give red-flowered offspring, some blues will give blue offspring and may give reds as well.

The ideal time to sow is in early spring, but without a propagating case you may have to wait until temperatures begin to rise. It is possible to sow seed at any time of the year, but it can be difficult to keep seedlings growing through the winter. If seed is purchased in the autumn it is best to place the packet in a refrigerator (not the freezing compartment) and store the seed there until you are ready to sow.

The seed is very fine: a packet of 50 seeds will appear to contain no more than a little dust. Use a preparatory seed-sowing compost, or potting compost mixed in equal parts with vermiculite in a half-size seed tray. Make sure the compost is moist before sowing.

Carefully open the packet and gently tap it so that the seed is scattered over the surface. Do not cover the seed with compost. Gently spray with water and cover with glass or polythene and place in a propagator or warm spot at a temperature of about 68°F (20°C) in bright light but not full sun.

Placing the seed tray under fluorescent lights is an ideal way of growing the young plants. Check regularly to ensure the surface of the compost is not drying out. Water again with a fine spray, as necessary. Probably the greatest cause of failure with seed is allowing it to dry out once it has started to germinate. Tiny plants should be visible after three to four weeks, but keep them enclosed for another two to three weeks to allow them to establish a proper root system. Gradually start to slide the glass or polythene cover off a little at a time: it should take about a week to get the cover right off.

It will take several more weeks for the seedlings to reach a size at which they can be transplanted. Once the leaves are large enough to handle, $\frac{1}{4}$ in. (5 to 6 mm), transplant each seedling into a very small pot of potting compost, or use a propagating cell pack and plant one seedling to each cell. The plants can be allowed to grow quite large, 4 in. (10 cm), before being knocked out of the pack and planted in a $3\frac{1}{2}$ in. (10 cm) pot.

Plants should flower within six months of sowing. From an early spring sowing you should have a good display of flowers during the first summer.

Plant Breeding

Great fun can be had by trying your luck at breeding new plants. There is always the possibility that you will hit on a winner. Although the chances are against it, at least you will know you have produced plants that are unique. A cross will usually give a great variation among the offspring; therefore, obviously the larger the numbers you grow, the greater the chance of success. Before making your cross, decide what you are aiming for. For example, are you looking for a multiflowered habit? If so, use a parent with that characteristic. The genetic make-up of streptocarpus is very complex. Even one characteristic, such as flower colour, is controlled by a range of genes. It is the mix of these genes that decides the colour. In addition, another series of genes is required for the colour to express itself. Yet another gene controls the presence of stripes on the petals. Thus you will understand that it is not easy to predict the colour, though generally blue is dominant over red, and the presence of stripes is dominant over the absence of stripes.

Remember, though, colour is not everything you need to look for. Other characteristics to consider in any new varieties are: length of the flower stalks, amount of flower, shape of the flowers, number of leaves, size of leaves, vigour of growth, disease resistance, temperature requirements and ease of propagation.

CROSS POLLINATION

To make a cross, take pollen containing the male sex cells from one plant and transfer it to the stigma of the female parent. Once on the stigma the pollen grows a tube down to the ovule in the ovary. Within the ovule is the female sex cell. The male sex cell passes down the pollen tube and fuses with the female sex cell as fertilisation takes place. Other cells also fuse and the ovule commences development into the seed. It is generally advisable to use the flower with the longer corolla tube as the pollen parent: its pollen will grow a longer pollen tube, more likely to reach the ovule, than pollen from a flower with a short corolla tube.

Select a flower bud on the plant that is to be the female parent

'Albatross' and 'Joanna' dominate a Chelsea display

29

when this bud is just at the point of opening. With a very sharp knife cut around the corolla tube and remove it, along with the stamens joined to it. This prevents the flower self-pollinating, as the anthers on the stamens will not have released any pollen at this stage. You will be left with just the female part of the flower. Take the ripe stamens – i.e. ones that have pollen on them (seen as a white powder) – from the pollen-parent flower and touch these on to the stigma of the emasculated flower. (A pair of forceps is useful in holding the stamens for this process.) Now fix a small plastic bag over the female flower using an elastic band. This prevents unwanted pollination occurring and prevents the exposed flower parts from drying out. To increase the chance of fertilisation occurring, after two days remove the plastic bag, repeat the pollination process on this same flower and the replace the plastic bag.

Be sure to keep a record of the cross and label the plant correspondingly. If the cross has taken, after a few weeks the ovary will start to elongate. The plastic bag can now be removed but mark the stem, for example by tying a piece of wool around it, so that you can recognise the developing fruit. After about two months, as the ovary ripens it will dry and darken and start to split open. Remove it from the plant and carefully shake the seed from it onto a piece of clean white paper. This seed is now ready for sowing. (See page 26.)

As the plants grow, watch for the appearance of desirable characteristics, as mentioned previously. Somewhere amongst the new plants may be the features you were hoping for, or there may be other attractive features that come as a surprise.

Often characteristics can remain hidden in this generation and only show up in the second generation, so do not give up if your plants are not what you wanted. Let them flower and self-pollinate, which they will do by themselves. Once again allow the seed pods to set, collect and sow the seed. Grow another set of plants. You may then be lucky with the next generation.

MUTATIONS

New variations also arise as mutations. A plant is made up of enormous numbers of microscopic cells. Each of these cells has within it a nucleus, and within this nucleus are thread-like structures called chromosomes which are made up of bands of information called genes. Mutations occur when the genes alter or the number of chromosomes in the nucleus of the cell varies. Mutations quite frequently occur naturally. They are most noticeable when the colour of the flower changes, but many other

'Sandra' and its red sport, 'Stella' (see p. 59)

characteristics can also change. The change can be quite dramatic or very small and subtle. As in growing plants from seed derived by making a cross, the chances are that the new forms may be interesting but of no great value. Sometimes, however, you may be lucky and find something worthwhile. Thus from 'Cynthia' has come 'Ruby'; from 'Sandra' has come 'Stella', and from 'Falling Stars' has come 'Gloria'.

If a plant has some different coloured flowers, follow the flower stalks down and you will find these are all joined to the base of one leaf. To grow plants with this new colour, take this leaf as cutting

material. The plants so derived will have flowers only of this new colour.

The rate at which mutations occur can be speeded up considerably in the laboratory by the use of chemicals and X-rays. A leaf is prepared as a cutting by removing the mid-rib as explained in the propagation chapter, on page 24. The cut face is immersed in a solution of colchicine for several hours. The leaf can then be planted in the usual way or treated with X-rays.

When new plants grow from the cut face of a leaf they do so from a single cell. Thus if any variation has occurred in the number of chromosomes, or in the genes on the chromosomes in that single cell, every cell derived from the original cell will carry that same variation.

X-rays damage the genes and so when a cell which has been exposed to X-rays grows into a plant this may well have variations from the normal. For example the length of the flower stalks may vary. This was how 'Mini Nymph' was derived from 'Constant Nymph'.

Colchicine stops cell division occurring properly and may give rise to cells that have double the normal complement of chromosomes, so-called tetraploids. So from a leaf thus treated a plant grows in which all the cells have this characteristic. Such plants can usually be seen quite clearly because they tend to be larger than normal. The leaves are broader and thicker, the flowers larger. 'Albatross' (see page 12) and 'Cobalt Nymph' are examples of this. Tetraploids do occur naturally sometimes, but they are generally no better than the normal plant. They may look rather coarse and lack the daintiness of the parent.

Above: Floriferous *Streptocarpus* 'Falling Stars' (see p. 54)

Below: *Streptocarpus* 'Gloria': a pink sport of 'Falling Stars' (see p. 54)

Showing

Streptocarpus have become very popular in recent years as show plants. There are often classes just for streptocarpus, but even if not they usually do well against other flowering plants in the open classes. The best time to show a plant is in its second year.

The first year should be used to build up a strong sturdy plant. A rooted cutting should be potted up into a 3½ in. (10 cm) pot early in the spring and grown steadily on. This will then be ready for potting into a 5 in. (13 cm) pot in about July. By the end of this first season the plant should be really stocky. Let it rest for the first part of the winter by keeping the temperature low (a minimum of 47°F/8°C), but as light levels start to increase in late January or early February bring the temperature up gradually to about 64°F (18°C) during the day and 59°F (15°C) at night. At the same time, begin feeding with a high potash feed, a little to start with and gradually increase the strength and frequency. Remove early flower buds but allow the flowers to develop when the show is ten to twelve weeks away. This time will vary somewhat with growing conditions, such as the state of the weather and the type of greenhouse in which the plants are housed. The time of year will also have an effect on the rate of flower development: the longer days and higher light levels of mid-summer will speed growth. Experience will determine the time for development in due course.

The plants chosen for showing should have a good, balanced head of leaves. Since the flowers grow from the bases of the leaves, the more leaves there are the more flowers there will be in due course. Keep the show plants well spaced apart so that they do not develop long leaves with drawn and spindly flower stems. Plants should never need to be staked – the flower stems should be self-supporting.

Aim for plants with leaves in good condition, preferably all perfect, though a little judicious trimming is permitted. The plants should have a large, well-balanced, rounded head of flowers.

Free-flowering cultivars (see pages 50–62) that make good show plants include 'Lisa', 'Ruby', 'Tina', 'Falling Stars', 'Gloria' and 'Paula'. The large-flowering cultivars, such as 'Susan' and 'Albatross', also make spectacular show plants. However, flowers are quite easily bruised if knocked around during transportation,

A Chelsea Flower Show display with 'Ruby' in the foreground and 'Falling Stars' behind

particularly those of large-flowered cultivars. Obviously, damaged flowers will lose marks.

When moving plants about do so carefully, making sure there is nothing for the flowers to knock against. Keep the plants well separated. Make sure the plants do not get too warm during transport as they bruise more easily at higher temperatures.

A group of free-flowering cultivars which includes 'Susan' in the foreground, 'Lisa', behind and S. *glandulosissimus* to the left

Diseases and Pests

Streptocarpus are easily grown and generally suffer little from diseases and pests, but one must be on the look-out and take the necessary action at the first sign of any trouble. The symptoms of the main diseases and pests are described below.

As new garden chemicals are introduced, so others are withdrawn. Because of these frequent changes it is best, once a problem is identified, to visit a garden centre and find a current control for that particular disease or pest.

Good growing conditions for plants and a lack of stress will keep pest and disease problems to a minimum, and if they do arise the spread of the problem will be slower. Good hygiene is of paramount importance. Compost must be sterile so that problems are not introduced from this source. Always use a reputable brand. Sterilise all previously used pots and propagation trays.

Always remove any plant debris so that fungi do not have a chance to grow and spread their spores. Weeds must not be allowed to become established as they may harbour pests and diseases which act as a reservoir, allowing the infection of your cultivated plants.

DISEASES

The best control of fungal diseases is preventative: get the growing conditions right.

- Avoid excessive sunlight which can damage the surface of the leaf, allowing infection to start.
- Always ensure there is adequate ventilation.
- Remember plants do not like to be kept cold and damp.
- Never overwater.

If plants are left standing in water, the roots cannot function because of lack of air in the compost; rot may start at the base of the plant, and the leaves wilt. (Do not confuse this with the plant wilting because it is too dry.) If the compost is wet and the plant wilts, let the compost dry out completely before giving it any more water. The plant may then recover.

- If just one or two leaves wilt, rot may be occurring at their bases; if they are given a pull they may come cleanly away, leaving the rest of the plant healthy.
- Remove any old and decaying material completely. Good hygiene eliminates the source of spores that would infect other plants.

Botrytis (Grey mould)

Botrytis occurs if leaves are left wet and cold, especially in winter. Grey fluffy growth may show, the leaf will rot away at the end or holes may develop in it. Break off any affected parts of the leaf. Do not allow any dead plant parts, such as the petals, to lie on the leaf as these will act as a source of infection. In a greenhouse, improve ventilation if the disease has appeared, and some additional heating may be required in winter.

Powdery mildew

Powdery mildew can occur on the leaves, the flowers or the flower stalks. The disease shows as whitish spots which gradually expand to form larger circles. Again, good air movement will help to prevent this disease. Powdery mildew is not usually a problem on streptocarpus, but will move on to them from more susceptible plants, such as saintpaulias. For some reason, purple-flowered streptocarpus seem more prone to the disease than other colours.

PESTS

Aphids (greenfly)

Like many pot plants, streptocarpus can be infected with these pests. Aphids that infest streptocarpus are small soft-bodied insects either green or orange in colour. They travel long distances on air currents, so that they seem to appear on the plants spontaneously. Once they arrive new generations are produced very rapidly. They are more likely to occur on plants that are stressed by frequently being allowed to become over-dry and wilted. The aphids may occur at the centre of the plant or on the flowers, the buds and their stalks. Often the most obvious symptom is the mass of tiny discarded white skins stuck onto the plant. These must not be confused with whitefly. If aphids occur on young plants, the leaves may be curled and distorted.

The individuals are all females that produce live young at a rate of three to six a day. These reach maturity within one week and themselves start producing offspring. Thus colonies rapidly build up. Some individuals will walk or fly to adjoining plants and so the process will begin again.

Aphids feed on the plant allowing a lot of the sweet sap that they imbibe to pass straight through their bodies; it is called honeydew. This forms a sticky layer on the leaves below. This sugary layer is food for unsightly black sooty mould which will grow on the leaves. Once the aphids are controlled, the sooty mould disappears as it runs out of honeydew.

Mealybugs

These pests may be easily missed as they are small, white, waxy, flattened insects that fix themselves alongside the veins on the underside of the leaves, where they suck the sap. Large colonies have the appearance of a white woolly mass.

Vine weevils

The vine weevil is wingless, about $\frac{3}{8}$ in. (9 mm) long, black with yellow speckling and a pointed head. It is common both outdoors and under glass. The adult chews notches in leaves. It is nocturnal, spending its days concealed under pots or in plant debris. Its eggs are laid near the base of a plant. The grubs that emerge are white with brown heads and are legless, up to $\frac{3}{10}$ in. (8 mm) long. They look like plump white maggots and chew into the base of the plant causing wilting and collapse.

Sciarid flies

These small black flies are about $\frac{1}{16}$ in. (2 mm) in length. They run about on the surface of the compost, and when disturbed fly off. The slender larvae are white with black heads; they may feed on root hairs and kill young plants and reduce the vigour of older plants. They live more frequently on peat and decaying matter and normally do not cause a problem.

Whiteflies

These are rarely found on streptocarpus. Whiteflies are more likely to develop and feed on other plants and merely rest on the streptocarpus. They are small white moth-like insects that will fly into the air with a characteristic jerky flight if disturbed.

Tarsonemid mites (cyclamen mites)

These mites are too small to be seen with the naked eye. The symptoms are distorted leaves that are often brown and rusty-looking at the base. The flowers are also distorted, hairy-looking, with a darker colour than usual and blotchy. There is no cure for these mites available to the amateur, although use of an insecticidal soap may control them to some extent. It is best to isolate any infested plants and, if necessary, destroy them before the mites spread onto other plants. Since the mites cannot fly, they can only move slowly from plant to plant, although they can stick on clothing and be moved about that way. Many pot plants beside streptocarpus are susceptible to these pests.

Thrips
Thrips are elongate insects $\frac{1}{16}$ in. (2 mm) long that will cause small pale blotches to occur on the flowers, and pollen to be shed from the anthers. They are very small, but can be seen as little torpedo-shaped yellowish/brown creatures if a flower is shaken onto a sheet of paper. Thrips are becoming very widespread.

Slugs
If the edges of the leaves or flowers are being eaten away and slime trails are visible, then the problem is caused by slugs. Normally these are not much of a nuisance except when conditions are suitable, such as under greenhouse benching where it is damp and shady. They are encouraged by rotting vegetation. Look at the affected plant, for the slug may well be found under a leaf, in the pot or under the base of the pot. It can easily be removed and destroyed.

Bumble bees
If a small hole is found at the base of the flowers, suspect bumble bees. Since these insects want to get at the nectar at the base of the flower, they will try to insert their proboscis down the corolla tube. They then find they cannot reach the nectar so they resort to puncturing a hole at the base of the corolla tube. There is little that can be done to prevent this damage except by somehow excluding these insects. This injury is fairly superficial, and of course is unlikely to occur to plants growing in a house.

BIOLOGICAL CONTROL

Biological controls are used commercially and are also available for amateur use for some of the above pests. This type of control relies on releasing a predator or parasite that will destroy the pest. These controls are preferable to chemical controls; they have no harmful environmental impact, they cannot harm the user or the plants, and the pest cannot become resistant. If you are growing plants in a greenhouse or conservatory, consider using biological controls. These controls are not as spectacular as chemical ones. There isn't an immediate knock-down effect, rather the pest gradually disappears. It may reappear later but again it will be dealt with by the predator. At first pests often tend to multiply more rapidly than the predators so that their numbers may build up before the predator can get control of them. A number of introductions of the predator may therefore be necessary. Biological controls rarely allow the complete eradication of a pest, but they do efficiently control pest numbers.

Biological controls will not work in winter when temperature and light levels are low, so some chemicals may be needed then. However, during the winter the multiplication rate of the pests themselves also slows down. Insecticidal soaps, and some other chemicals, can be used without harming the predators used in biological control. The use of biological agents and compatible pesticides is known as 'integrated pest management'.

It is best to begin all these biological controls as soon as pests are seen. Do not let the pest build up to plague proportions before starting, as the predator may then be unable to get control of the situation. Regular monitoring is vital: hang yellow or blue sticky traps amongst the plants to enable you to spot the arrival of pests such as thrips and sciarid flies before you might otherwise spot them on the plants.

As anxiety about using chemical pesticides increases, and more chemicals are withdrawn from the market, the use of preventative measures and biological control will become increasingly important.

Biological controls are available for the following pests.

Aphid control
The control for aphids is a small black wasp, about $\frac{1}{16}$ in. (2 mm) long, called *Aphidius*. It feeds on honeydew (the excess plant sap excreted by the aphid) or nectar. It lays its eggs in the bodies of young aphids. The eggs hatch producing larvae that feed within the body of the aphid. When the larvae are ready to pupate they cut a slit in the body of the aphid and fix it to the leaf surface by a silk thread. Each larva then spins a silken cocoon and metamorphoses into the adult form. At this time the aphid becomes swollen up and yellow in colour. The adult *Aphidius* can lay up to a hundred eggs. Introduce *Aphidius* every few weeks at a rate of about five per square yard/metre.

Aphids can also be controlled by a midge, *Aphidoletes aphidimyza*. This small fly lays its eggs on plants infested by aphids, and from these eggs larvae emerge that feed on the aphids. *Aphidoletes* can be obtained as the pupae in a carrier material which is placed amongst infested plants. Once the adults develop, they actively seek out infested plants. These midges live on aphids and are not the same as those that attack humans.

Vine weevil control

A nematode (round worm) has proved effective against vine weevil larvae. The nematode enters its host through body openings. Once inside it releases bacteria that multiply and form food for the nematode. The nematode is then able to reproduce. About two days later the vine weevil larva dies and the nematode leaves to find new hosts. Nematodes are available as a preparation that can be mixed with water which is then applied to the soil. It is best used in late summer before vine weevil grubs have grown large enough to cause serious damage.

Sciarid flies

The nematodes that control vine weevils can also be used against sciarid fly larvae.

Thrip control

Amblyseius is a small mite that is a very effective predator of thrips. These mites are very active and spread amongst the plants. Both the adults and their young consume two to five thrips each per day.

Amblyseius is produced on bran or vermiculite which is supplied to customers. The infested bran or vermiculite is then sprinkled onto the plants.

Mealybug control

A ladybird beetle called *Cryptolaemus montrouzieri* will attack mealybugs. The adult beetle is black and orange, about 4 mm long. It lays its eggs in the mealybug colonies and these eggs hatch out into larvae that grow to ½ in (1 cm) in size and look like overgrown mealybugs. Both adults and larvae feed on all stages of the mealybug. Introduce one *Cryptolaemus* for every three mealybug infected plants.

GROWTH MALFORMATIONS

Occasionally the growing regions of two adjoining flowers fail to separate. This leads to a stalk of double thickness surmounted by a rather gross flower made of two flowers joined laterally. Similar malformed growth also occurs with leaves, resulting in a leaf made up of three or four half leaves joined along a common mid-rib. This type of malformation is known as 'fasciation'. It occurs more frequently in some varieties than others, for example 'Wiesmoor Red'. If the offending parts are removed, the rest of the plant will carry on growing normally.

SUPPLIERS OF BIOLOGICAL CONTROLS

Defenders Ltd, Freepost, PO Box 131, Wye, Ashford, Kent TN25 5TQ.

English Woodlands Biocontrol, Graffham, Petworth, Sussex GU28 0LR.

Green Gardener Products, 41 Strumpshaw Road, Norwich NR13 5OG.

Natural Pest Control (Amateur), Watermead, Yapton Road, Barnham, Bognor Regis, West Sussex PO2 0BQ.

Wye Bugs, Wye College, Ashford, Kent TN25 5AH.

All the above supply biological controls for spider mites, mealybugs, thrips and aphids; all except Natural Pest Control supply the vine weevil nematode. The slug nematode is available from Defenders.

Biological controls can also be purchased through garden centres as Zeneca; Nature's Friends for controlling spider mites, aphids, vine weevil and slugs, as appropriate.

A Selection of Species

Species are wild plants and not of garden origin. They should not be ignored, however. They may not be as flamboyant as some hybrids, but they can be very delicate and quite delightful.

Variation, such as flower colour, can occur within a species. Confusion can also be caused by naturally occurring inter-specific crosses, leading to forms intermediate between the parents.

STEMMED STREPTOCARPUS (Sub-genus *Streptocarpella*)

There are over 40 of these stemmed species.

S. caulescens An upright plant growing to 20 in. (50 cm) in height. The stem is a rich brown colour. The flowers develop in the axils of the leaves (the point where the leaves meet the stem) near to the apex, and grow above it. The flowers are small, $\frac{3}{4}$ in. (2 cm), but produced in large numbers in a deep purple. The effect is superficially like a mass of violets in full bloom.

S. caulescens var. pallescens This is similar to the above but lacks the strong pigments. The stem is green and the flowers are white or pale violet with darker violet lines.

S. glandulosissimus This is a lax, straggling plant of the mountain rain-forests. A single plant can cover a large area. It can be grown to particularly good advantage in a hanging basket, where it will cascade over the sides to produce a very striking effect. The flowers are small and violet-blue. The plant is sometimes an epiphyte, i.e. it grows on the surface of trees, gaining a positional advantage.

S. saxorum Another straggling species that is best grown in a hanging basket. The leaves are fleshy and blue-green in colour. The flowers are pale blue, about 1.5 in. (3.5 cm) long, held well clear of the stems on long thin flower stalks. The species varies in form somewhat, some varieties being more compact than others and having a more upright habit. In the wild S. *saxorum* grows on rock faces and cliffs, in a position often fully exposed to the sun but

Above: *Streptocarpus caulescens*
Below: *Streptocarpus glandulosissimus*

Streptocarpus cyanandrus (see p. 47)

where mist occurs. Thus, in cultivation it requires a bright position, and can be kept flowering for most of the year. This species is an excellent pot plant and is probably the best stemmed streptocarpus for the average grower.

ROSULATES (the rosette habit)
(Sub-genus *Streptocarpus*)

S. candidus This grows to become a large plant with leaves up to 24 by 8 in. (60 by 20 cm). The flowers are fairly small, 1½ in. (4 cm), but each inflorescence has up to 25 flowers, and many inflorescences may be flowering at one time so the total effect is quite spectacular. The flowers are white with two violet-blue chevrons on the base of the corolla. Flowering occurs in flushes, each flush lasting for about two months. One of the very few scented streptocarpus, the flowers have a very pleasant honey scent, especially noticeable on warm days. This streptocarpus is a delightful plant when in full flower and is well worth growing. (See page 25.)

S. cyanandrus A very small plant with leaves growing to about 2½ in. (6 cm). The flowers are also small, 1¼ in. (3 cm). The interesting thing about the plant is the presence of purple pigments. The leaves are tinged purple and the flowers are pale magenta-pink with darker magenta-pink stripes. After flowering at quite an early age the plant dies.

This is an attractive little plant, but is certainly not the easiest to grow. Grow in a small pot and do not allow it to dry out nor be subjected to strong sunlight. It is best propagated by seed.

S. cyaneus A medium-sized plant with leaves about 12 in. (30 cm) long. The flowers are rose-pink with a distinct yellow band in the base, flanked by deeper pink streaks. (See page 48.)

S. fanniniae A large plant with bright green leaves. The flowers are produced in large numbers, pale blue with purple markings on the lower half. They have a very slight scent. It grows in damp situations in the wild, such as marshy stream banks, and because of this the plant has large, thin leaves and needs much more water than many other streptocarpus.

S. gardenii A small neat plant. The leaves are strap-shaped, about 8 in. (20 cm) in length. The most characteristic feature of the plant is the flower colour, greenish white with violet lines. It bears one or two flowers per stalk.

S. johannis This is the plant that has given the multi-flowered inflorescences to many of the modern hybrids. There may be 12 or more flowers per stalk. The flowers are small and pale blue in colour, the inflorescence 12 in. (30 cm) or more in height.

S. primulifolius subsp. formosus The flowers of this plant are large, up to 4 in. (10 cm) in length, with one or two per inflorescence. The colour is pale mauve, the throat yellow with purple spotting. This is a very lovely plant and is well worth a place in a streptocarpus collection. It is one of the parents of 'Sandra' which has a very similar habit. (See page 59.)

DIBLEYS NURSERIES

Streptocarpus
cyaneus

S. rexii This compact, neat plant is the type on which modern hybrids are based. The flowers are white or pale violet with seven distinct violet stripes in the corolla. This species occurs further south-west in Africa than any other, nearer to Cape Town, hence its discovery in 1818, earlier than any other streptocarpus.

UNIFOLIATES (plants with a single leaf)

S. dunnii Although, as explained earlier, the unifoliates are not worth growing except by the keen gardener, this one is included because it is quite different in colour from any other *Streptocarpus* species and has played such an important part in giving the beautiful reds to modern hybrids. The mass of small flowers are rose to deep crimson in colour and make a striking sight. The single leaf is about 12 in. (30 cm) in length. The plant is monocarpic: this means it only flowers once before dying.

Opposite: *Streptocarpus cyaneus* (see p. 47)
Below: *Streptocarpus dunnii*

— Streptocarpus of Garden Origin —

Where known, the breeder's name is placed in parenthesis after the description. Plants marked 'AGM' were given an Award of Garden Merit at the Royal Horticultural Society trials at Wisley Garden in 1992.

'Albatross' Being a tetraploid, it is a strong broad-leaved plant. Flowers are pure white with a yellow centre. A well-grown plant is very striking. (See page 28.) (Broertjes) AGM

'Amanda' The flowers are rich blue with darker veining and a white throat. The inflorescence stalks are short and upright, giving a tight round head of flowers. (Dibleys')

'Anne' The flowers are fully double, in deepest purple. The colour is derived from one of its parents, 'Elsi'; and the double habit comes from its other parent, 'Rosebud'. (Dibleys')

'Athena' A small compact plant, with masses of flowers on short stalks. The colour is white with a hint of pink and, with red stripes in the throat. This is one of the smallest of the cultivars and, if space is limited, is a most suitable plant. 'Athena' was bred in the USA. (See page 14.)

Streptocarpus 'Anne' (see above)

Streptocarpus 'Amanda' (see p. 50)

'Beryl' This has a neat upright habit. The flowers are white with deep purple veining. 'Beryl' is a white sport of 'Heidi'. (Dibleys')

'Blue Gem' Another small plant suitable for narrow window sills. Neat in habit, the flowers are pale blue with a yellow eye, held on short stalks. (Brown)

'Blue Heaven' A compact variety from the United States. The many dainty lavender-blue semi-double flowers are medium in size and are round and wavy in shape. (Ford)

'Blue Nymph' This is one of the Dutch variations of 'Constant Nymph'. The flowers are sky blue with pencilling and a creamy throat. (Broertjes)

'Carol' The flowers of 'Carol' have a different shape from all the other named varieties in that the petals are wavy. Very free flowering. The flowers are deep pink with a white and yellow throat. (Dibleys')

Streptocarpus 'Beryl' (see p. 51)

'Chorus Line' A plant of similar habit and flower type as 'Blue Heaven'. The double flower is white with an attractive network of purple veining on the lower half. (Ford)

'Cobalt Nymph' This mutant of 'Constant Nymph' produced by combined colchicine and X-ray treatment. It is a tetraploid, which causes it to have strong thick leaves, rigid upright flower stems and flowers larger than its parent. As the name suggests the colour is cobalt blue. (Broertjes)

'Concord Blue' Quite different from all the other hybrids listed here in that this is a *Streptocarpella* (i.e. stemmed) hybrid. A bushy plant with small rounded leaves and a head of small blue flowers.

'Constant Nymph' This plant marks a milestone in the breeding of modern streptocarpus. The first multi-flowered plant was developed at the John Innes Institute and introduced in 1947. A fairly large plant with long flower stalks. The flowers are violet-blue with deeper violet veins and with a creamy yellow throat. (Lawrence)

'Cynthia' A free-flowering plant with flowers of a brilliant glowing magenta with darker markings in the centre. One of its parents is 'Tina', and from this it inherits a good sturdy habit. (Brown) AGM

'Diana' One of the 1973 John Innes hybrids. Deep cerise with a white throat.

Streptocarpus 'Chorus Line' (see p. 52)

'**Eira**' In Welsh 'eira' means snow and this sums up the colour of the flowers, white with just a hint of mauve on the lower petals. The flowers are small but produced in masses and are semi-double in form. It is not a vigorous grower. (Brown)

'**Elsi**' The colour of this plant is spectacular: deepest purple almost bordering on black, with two small yellow streaks in the throat. The flowers are held upright.

'**Falling Stars**' This is the most floriferous of any streptocarpus. It is a sport of S. *johannis*, but it has shorter inflorescence stalks than the species and is a deeper blue. It is strong-growing and easily propagated. A well-grown plant of 'Falling Stars' can have literally hundreds of flowers. The flowers are small, about ¾ in. (2 cm) across. This variety is the basis of a new range of small-flowered floriferous hybrids. It is a must for any collection. (Dibleys') AGM

'**Festival Wales**' Introduced in 1992, it was named to commemorate the Garden Festival held at Ebbw Vale that year. It has large flowers that are pale purple at the top shading to a rich deep purple on the lower petals. A very beautiful plant. (Dibleys')

'**Fiona**' A John Innes introduction. Lax trusses of pink flowers are produced very freely.

'**Gloria**' This very dainty plant is a pink sport of 'Falling Stars'. It is identical to it in every way except that the flowers are pale pink with slightly darker pencilling, and it is just as free-flowering. (Dibleys') AGM

'**Happy Snappy**' A new hybrid from the USA. It is a compact plant with flowers in a bright red with no hint of blue in them.

'**Heidi**' The leaves stay reasonably short and the flowers are held upright giving a neat appearance. These flowers are a lovely clear blue with deep purple markings on the lower petals; the inflorescences only have a few flowers each. AGM

'**Helen**' Pastel blue flowers are very freely borne. Leaves are characteristically dark green. (John Innes Institute) AGM

'**Joanna**' Very vigorous and grows to form a large plant. The flowers are the deepest red of any variety. The petals have a velvety appearance, the lower ones with deeper markings than the upper. (Brown) (See pages 1 and 28.)

'**Julie**' A medium-sized plant with a nice upright head of flowers that have a rounded face; colour is rosy pink with cyclamen/purple markings extending into a yellow throat. (Dibleys')

Above: *Streptocarpus* 'Fiona', one of the original John Innes hybrids (see p. 54)
Below: *Streptocarpus* 'Heidi (see p. 54); with fairly short leaves and upright growing flowers, this makes a compact plant

'**Karen**' The flowers are a drab magenta-red in colour, but there are now better reds than this. (John Innes Institute)

'**Kim**' Another small compact plant. The leaves never grow very long and the inflorescence stalks are short. Multiflowered heads of small flowers, freely produced, in a deep inky blue colour. Deservedly a popular plant. (Dibleys') AGM (See page 4.)

'**Lisa**' Very free-flowering in a delicate shell pink with a white eye. A well-grown plant of 'Lisa' can produce a solid head of flowers 18 in. (45 cm) across. (See page 21.) (Dibleys') AGM

'**Louise**' Blue with yellow streaks on the lower petals, but now superseded by better blues. (John Innes Institute)

'**Lynne**' A short plant with rich velvety purple flowers that unusually have a black eye. (Dibleys')

'**Margaret**' The flowers are small and upturned, violet-blue in colour with deeper veining. They are carried on very long stalks. The real virtue of the plant is that it will continue to flower through the short days of winter, provided the temperature is high enough. Others with this useful characteristic are being developed. (John Innes Institute)

'**Maassen's White**' This is the white form of 'Constant Nymph' which it resembles in every way, except that it has lost all blue pigment. The stalks are green and the flowers pure white with a yellow eye. (Maassen)

'**Marie**' This is a compact plant with an upright head of flowers that are dusky purple in colour with a white throat. (John Innes Institute)

'**Merton Blue**' A large-flowering blue variety that was crossed with S. johannis to give the multi-flowered 'Constant Nymph'. (John Innes Institute)

'**Mini Nymph**' A compact form of 'Constant Nymph'. The flowers are identical, but the plant has shorter leaves and flower stems, making it an improved cultivar. (Broertjes)

'**Neptune**' A variety of the older type with a few large flowers on each stalk. The flowers are blue with a yellow throat. Although there are better varieties, it is still often available.

Above: *Streptocarpus* 'Nicola' (see p. 58)
Below: *Streptocarpus* 'Sally' (see p. 58)

'Nicola' Both the leaves and the flowers are held upright. It has masses of small deep pink flowers, many being semi-double (i.e. some of the stamens in the flowers develop as small petals). (Brown)

'Olga' Flowers are a rose pink colour with darker markings. The colour is not dissimilar to 'Tina', but the flowers are not so freely produced and the habit is not as good. (John Innes Institute)

'Paula' Quite a large plant. The flowers are reddish purple, the lower petals darker with distinct veining into a yellow throat. (See page 10.) (John Innes Institute) AGM

'Rosebud' This first fully double streptocarpus was bred in the United States. The plant is large and robust, the deep pink flowers are also big, deeply ruffled with a cluster of extra petals at the centre. The first flowers sometimes tend to be single, and at times the lower petals fail to open properly. 'Rosebud' is something quite new and distinct. (See page 14.)

'Ruby' This excellent medium-sized, very free-flowering plant is a sport of 'Cynthia'. It has lost the blue tinge in the magenta flowers leaving them a lovely rich ruby-red colour. (See page 16.) (Dibleys') AGM

'Sally' The plant has a neat compact habit and is another in the series of fully double flowers. The edges of the petals are frilly, the colour a clear blue. (Dibleys')

Streptocarpus 'Sandra' (see p. 59)

Streptocarpus 'Stella' (see below)

'Sandra' One of the parents is S. *primulifolius* subsp. *formosus* and the flowers are similar to this species in form, but their colour is a much deeper mauve with a tracery of deep purple veining on the lower petals, leading into a yellow throat. (See page 31.) (Brown)

'Sarah' A plant with the same habit and flower type as 'Sandra', but of a darker, richer purple. (Dibleys') AGM

'Snow White' This Dutch-induced mutation of 'Maassen's White', is quite distinct from all others in flower form. The plant is small and neat, and therefore best grown in a smaller pot than is usual for other streptocarpus: 3 in. (9 cm) for first-year plants. Leaves are no longer than 6 in. (15 cm) and though there are few flowers per inflorescence, it is nevertheless very floriferous. The colour is the same as the parent, white with a yellow eye, but the flower is small and upturned, resembling a freesia in form. This plant will flower very early in the year, but is more prone to rot in the winter if it gets too cool and damp; it is happier if the temperature can be kept to a minimum of 50°F (10°C). (See page 12.) (Broertjes) AGM

'Stella' A sport from 'Sandra'; identical to it except that it has lost the blue coloration, turning the purple flower into a very nice pink with plum red veining. (See page 31.) (Dibleys') AGM

'Susan' Medium-length leaves, and flowers that are larger than the John Innes type, with few flowers per inflorescence. It is a striking plant when in flower; the habit is compact, the flowers intense magenta with a marked yellow centre. (Dibleys') AGM

Above: *Streptocarpus* 'Susan' (see p. 59), with large, brilliantly coloured flowers and medium sized leaves
Below: *Streptocarpus* 'Tina', one of the best of the John Innes hybrids (see p. 61)

Streptocarpus 'Tracey' (see below)

'Tina' Probably the best streptocarpus from the John Innes Institute and a plant well worth growing. It is excellent, compact, vigorous and propagates easily. The flowers are pink on the upper petals and the lower petals bright magenta with distinct veins. A well-grown plant is really striking and can have a solid head of flowers 12 in. (30 cm) or more across. (See also front cover.) (John Innes Institute)

'Tracey' A medium-sized plant with strong upright flower stalks carrying a multi-flowered head of small deep magenta flowers. These flowers are similar in size to 'Falling Stars', $\frac{3}{4}$ in. (2 cm). (Dibleys')

'Wiesmoor Red' This is a plant of the old *S. × hybridus* type, i.e. it has only one or two large flowers per inflorescence and these are long and trumpet-shaped. However, the colour is a very deep red. The leaves remain short but tend to die back at the ends, giving a ragged appearance. When in flower the plant resembles a florist's gloxinia. 'Wiesmoor Red' is one variety selected from a range of colours obtained from Wiesmoor Hybrids seed mix. (Benary)

'Winifred' This has large numbers of small delicate mauve/blue flowers which are semi-double in form, and carried on rigid upright stalks. (Brown)

Further Information

RECOMMENDED READING

Virginie, F. and George A. Elbert, *The Miracle Houseplants*. Crown Publishers, Inc., New York, 1984.

O. M. Hilliard and B. L. Burtt, *Streptocarpus, An African Plant Study*. University of Natal Press, 1971.

Garden Chemicals, a guide to their safe and effective use, a booklet which gives information on the correct use of current pesticides, can be obtained from the British Agrochemical Association, 4 Lincoln Court, Lincoln Road, Peterborough PE1 2R.

SOCIETIES

American Gloxinia and Gesneriad Society, Inc., 399 River Road, Hudson, MA 01799–2627, USA.

The Saintpaulia and Houseplant Society, 33 Church Road, Newbury Park, Ilford, Essex IG2 7ET.

SUPPLIERS OF STREPTOCARPUS

Dibleys' Nurseries, Llanelidan, Ruthin, N. Wales LL15 2LG.
Large range of hybrids and species

Uzumara Orchids, 9 Port Henderson, Gairloch, Ross-shire IV21 2AS.
Species

Streptocarpus seeds are available from most leading seedsmen.

Index

Page numbers in **bold** refer to illustrations